Get Your Life Back

Addiction Workbook

By Don Mingo

Mingo Coaching Group LLC, Big Bend, Wisconsin.

Cover Photo by Simone Acquaroli

ISBN-13: 978-1-7323525-2-0

DEDICATION

To you, the reader, and the millions struggling with addictions, habits, and bondages holding you hostage to a better life, this journal is dedicated to you. May you overcome that which detracts you from growing into that you desire to become.

*"Don't copy the behavior and customs of this world,
but let God transform you
into a new person
by changing the way you think.
Then you will learn to know
God's will for you,
which is good and pleasing and perfect."*[1]

B.A.C.K.S.®

Welcome to the Getting Your Life Back Journal! This journal is based upon the B.A.C.K.S.® system of Mind Renewal spoke of in Romans 12:2, "Don't copy the behavior and customs of this world, but let God transform you into a new person by **changing the way you think.** Then you will learn to know God's will for you, which is good and pleasing and perfect."

Changing the way you think about your problems, struggles, or bondage, is absolutely necessary to gain victory over that weight that slows you down, especially the struggle that so easily trips you up.[2]

B.A.C.K.S.???

Many ask, "Why the acronym "B.A.C.K.S.?" Twenty years of my adult life were spent living in Northern Natal, South Africa. The Zulu people make up the predominate population group in that area. Zulus number more than 5 million in Southern Africa. Learning the Zulu language, culture, and people proved both a rich and challenging experience.

Zulu is a language of clicks. It's full of picturesque proverbs. The Zulu people are a storytelling people. Often, they speak in proverbs, sages, and clichés. One such cliché heard often when describing a high expense of an action, item, or service was:

KUMBE EQOLO

"Kumbe" to dig, and "eqolo" into the lower back, literally means, "It's very expensive." Eqolo is at the base of the lower back. It's in the lower lumbar disc area of the posterior. What makes "eqolo" unique is the "q" click. The "q" is a palatal click of the tongue when spoken. Zulu people often use the phrase to describe a wide array of emotions towards something deemed too high a price. While learning the language, a Zulu speaker translated this phrase into broken English,

"It Digs the BACKS"

The phrase used many times by Zulus during our two decades in Northern Natal, South Africa carried a vast range of applications. A highly educated Zulu professional described the phrase as, **"Something which costs more than one can possibly anticipate."** Our addictions often cost us "Kumbe aqolo." They take one deeper into destruction of self, relationships, and integrity than ever imaged in the beginning.

Whatever your bondage or affliction, it probably costs you more than you ever anticipated. This is the nature of addiction. Addiction takes one farther downward into destructive spirals than ever expected.

B.A.C.K.S.® is an acronym for Boundaries, Accountability, Confession, Knowledge, and Sorrow. It's a soul-mind renewing process. Getting Your Life BACK Journal is a companion to my book, *Boundaries – Five Steps to Getting Your Life BACK.*

Why are addictions such a problem? During many sessions of listening to people struggling with various addictions, or sins, several common factors emerged. These factors are partly upon which B.A.C.K.S. is based.

Boundaries

First, few **Boundaries** preventing access to their addictions functioned well. If barriers existed at all, they were porous at best. An extremely high percentage of people gained access to whatever was ailing them. A sliver of availability always appeared when temptation's urge presented itself. "I tried." Or, "It wasn't my fault." Or, "I just couldn't resist," often waited on the other side of addiction's availability. Defenses constantly proved inadequate. A conditioned mind always provided paths to access.

Accountability

Accountability plans and partners were porous too. Oh, they enlisted accountability partners. Prepared plans to prevent addiction's accesses existed. But, their lifeboat continually took on water due to its lack of integrity. Doctors' instructions were regularly ignored. "What did your doctor say," I asked. "Well, they said to do this or that . . . but, I don't agree with them." Prescribed medications were misused, abused, or not taken. Also, accountability partners proved weak, inconsistent, and at times enabling. Often, accountability meant sitting with another equally struggling person suffering the same malady, both together excusing each other's for their deficits.

When it came to the Bible, many Christians participated in a haphazard practice of Scripture reading, if they read the Bible at all. Studies show a high percentage of Christians rarely read the Bible. Amazingly, with Scriptures readily available on varieties of media; Bible illiteracy is extremely high. Sadly, one of the most powerful weapons in a person's arsenal to overcome bondage is ignored. "For the word of God is alive and powerful . . . It exposes our innermost thoughts and desires" (Hebrews 4:12).

Confession

Confession, one of the highest attitude-changing disciplines of the Bible, was rarely practiced. While regrets were plenteous, confession didn't exist. "I'm so sorry . . ." accompanied many tears. Yet, one of two extremes often prevailed. Self-loathing or self-victimization became the mantra. Either, "I hate myself—I'm worthless," or "It's not my fault—I can't help myself," is the tag many hide behind to counter shame.

The art of biblical confession is little understood today by the Church. It's transforming power is rarely attempted. Often seen as merely penitence and punishment, its transformational power is experienced by marginally few. Confessions are usually weak attempts at prayer to an unknown Person one claims to believe in. "God, you know I've got this problem. I can't help myself. Help me help me. Amen." Or, conversely, "God, I'm such a crumb. I'd be better off dead." Neither extreme examples biblical confession and its renewing power. In Confession is Renewal!

Knowledge

Knowledge and understanding of the far-reaching tentacles of bondage's consequences went unexplored. Many explaining their plight, simply did not understand the costs of their captivity. Little understanding existed of the process taking place in their addiction through their addiction. Clueless to the damage done to countless people around them and themselves, ignorance was not bliss. It was rather blistering.

Sorrow

While self-loathing, excusing, guilt, or victimization abounded, few showed true "godly sorrow" for their decisions, habits, and actions. Godly **Sorrow** is the final key to getting your life back. Godly sorrow is different from guilt. It ensures victory. When one feels the way, God feels about their addiction, transforming recovery is within reach.

Getting Your Life Back depends on understanding and applying these principles. This five-step B.A.C.K.S. approach offered in the following pages emerges from assisting countless people over the years. It's a five-step process that can change your life! It's practical. It's understandable. It's mind changing. It's heart altering. And, it can salvage a damaged soul.

BACKS present a spiritual, cognitive, soul renewing process to help you in conjunction with your current approaches. Through a spiritual truth mind renewing process, B.A.C.K.S. helps change one's spiritual and cognitive thinking about issues driving them towards their addictions in the first place. Through the Holy Spirit's help, renewing of your mind, and changing your practices freedom can be grasped.

B.A.C.K.S.®

Boundaries –

Crossing into unhealthy boundaries opens people to the snares that enslave them into addictions, whether drug, opiates, media, alcohol, pornography, or others. Helping you see your unhealthy boundaries and begin deconstructing those boundaries is key in B.A.C.K.S.

Accountability –

Two deficits mark the biggest culprit's addictions' downward spirals. First, no time or thought is given to think about your condition. Just keep ignoring. Plow ahead. Today is tomorrow. Accountability means building a team around you to help you construct, recover, live, and stay within healthy boundaries.

Confession –

Sure, you've prayed. Your praying. Perhaps, you're begging God for help. But, prayer isn't working. What's the cause of unanswered prayer? True sound Bible confession is the answer to this dilemma.

Confession often carries only a connotation of penance, guilt, and negativity. Many share, "I tried praying about this, it doesn't work. Getting Your Life Back Journal seeks to help you develop deep soul-confessional disciplines. In true confession is freedom.

Knowledge –

How does your struggle affect your person, mind, and soul? What is the cost of an addiction? How does that addiction affect your soul, person, health, relationships, and people around you?

Repeatedly, people struggling with bondages enter their battle arenas untrained, unarmed, ill informed, and poorly prepared. Is it no wonder cravings holds so much power? Knowledge seeks to equip you with an understanding of the cost of your compulsions, and a way forward out of those habits.

Sorrow –

Worldly sorrow slays its victims continuously. Self-hating, guilt, self-loathing, feeling horrible about one's self debilitates functionality. Worldly guilt prohibits us from becoming the person created in the image of God. Seeing ourselves the way God sees us in our struggles is key to overcoming addiction.

Transformational Practices

Three transformational practices in this journal will help you begin to change the way you think about your struggle. Until your mind thinks differently about your addiction, it is my opinion that regardless of treatment, you will struggle to overcome. These 3 practices are:

Meditations

Ponderings

Prayer to Pray

Give it a try. Work at it. It's a start. At first, you'll perhaps feel clumsy. Keep working at it until it becomes a habit. Prayer transforms how one thinks.

Meditations

Reflect upon all the Scriptures, wise sayings, and quotes. Study them. Learn them. Think about them. The Word of God, the Bible, contains power towards changing your mind into rethinking in a healthier way.

> *"Thank God! He gives us victory over sin and death through our Lord Jesus Christ."*
> (1 Corinthians 15:57) GWT

Ponderings

Spend considerable time on Ponderings. Write your thoughts down. Write out your reflections. I beg you, please do not skip over them. Talk with yourself. Meditate, think, ponder, and muse. Working through Ponderings helps you battle the war going on in your mind affecting your thinking and actions. Ponderings helps bring transformation. Wander into pondering paths of challenge, discovery, correction, and connection.

A Prayer to Pray

Pray each prayer with your whole heart. Learn to approach God during your times of deepest need. Experience God's love and acceptance. Here's your biggest supporter. Through prayer you will find God's availability in your times of deepest failures and fear. Learn to lean on Him experiencing his love and concern for you.

> *So let us come boldly to the throne of our gracious God.*
> *There we will receive his mercy,*
> *and **we will find grace to help us when we need it most**.*
> (Hebrews 4:16)

Here's the Thing about Dragons

"It does not do to leave a live dragon out of your calculations
if you live near him."

Gandalf
J. R. R. Tolkien – The Hobbit

An addiction sort of resembles a dragon. At least to me. Dragons are not real, of course, but let's pretend they are for a few moments, and you will soon get the connection. This chapter is not long, but you don't want to skip it. A dragon, when first acquired, is like most infant animals: they're cute. My step-dad once acquired a cute puppy that grew into a huge mammoth beast. The half German Shephard-Doberman once ripped his custom van to shreds after only leaving the dog alone in the vehicle for fifteen minutes. The dog did $6,000 worth of damage to his beloved vehicle.

Dragons are like that too. Young dragons are not that much trouble, not that much trouble at all; at first. They are easily kept hidden away and taken out when you want to play. They are so small you barely notice. They understand your needs. A newly acquired dragon is there for you. It heeds your every call. Controllability is a major advantage of owning a young dragon. You can take it out and put it away at the most convenient of times.

A young dragon provides many benefits. They're mythical, or so it seems, taking you to fantasies never imagined. A dragon takes you on exciting voyages. Exciting, deep, dark, exotic places await you – places you didn't know existed. Your young dragon offers unconditional acceptance, too, at least in the beginning. And this little fellow will take you just about anywhere you want to go, when you want to go, and whenever you want to go for as long as you want to stay.

Acceptance is a young dragon's greatest virtue. Your dragon accepts you just the way you are. There are no conditions. There are no responsibilities. You may present yourself any way you like.

Whether in a bad mood and a bit grumpy, you're accepted. Are you happy and excited? Perfect! There's no nagging, no fault finding, no conditions. Yes, you can just be you. There are zero entanglements! None of the problems that plague relationships present themselves in the beginning. No fuss, no mess, no problem – whatever you want. Your only responsibility is to you and your young dragon. Once you gain access to the dragon's world, it's free sailing from there! No arguments – none of that "my needs, your needs" stuff. No "my time your time" – none of that. No! It's a no-hassle relationship! No arguments! No in-laws! No family! No problems! It's up to you. Total control! It appears perfect in every way.

The cost of a relationship with your dragon, in the beginning, is minimal. There isn't a lot of money to lay out. There is no cost commitment. There is no spending on anything or anyone except yourself. But, perhaps best of all, there are zero relational struggles and hassles.

Also, you can treat your dragon in any manner you wish. Speak kindly. Speak harshly. Use the dragon. Abuse the dragon. Accuse the dragon. Neglect the dragon. Not a problem. In the beginning, your dragon is just happy to spend time, any time, with you. You are special.

A small dragon is a perfect companion. It introduces you to other wonderful companions. Your new dragon-friends enjoy your company. These new friends appear the most beautiful compliant people you've ever met. And here's the thing – they find you beautiful in every way. In fact, they love you, want you, and accept you just the way you are. Their only purpose is to serve and love you. Your dragon's mission's statement is:

"To Serve You, To Love You – That is All I Do."

It gives, expecting nothing in return; at least in the beginning. It's almost too good to be true. Yes, a young dragon seems perfect in every way. It's a wonder to behold. Dragons are quite the rage these days. It seems everybody has one, two, or three of them. Then, however, they start to grow. That's when trouble starts. That's when it begins to take control of your life exacting an ever-increasing price. That's when your DRAGON grows into an uncontrollable destructive eight-story building.

"Dragon" is our code word for Addiction, Habit, Bondage, or Problem

When you see the word **"dragon"**
it refers to porn, drugs, opioids, alcohol, media, or any other habit troubling you.

We will talk about your **dragon** much.

_____

_____

_____

_____

_____

Meditation

> *"I plead with you to give your bodies to God because of all he has done for you.*
> *Let them be a living and holy sacrifice – the kind he will*
> *find acceptable. This is truly the way to worship him.*
> *Don't copy the behavior and customs of this world,*
> *but let God transform you into a new person by changing the way you think.*
> *Then you will learn*
> *to know God's will for you, which is good and pleasing and perfect."*
> (Romans 12:1-2).

Ponderings

1. How did you first meet your dragon? _____

_____

_____

_____

_____

_____

_____

2. How long have you been together? _____

_____

_____

_____

3. What was your relationship like in the beginning? _____

_____

_____

_____

_____

_____

4. Describe your relationship now. _____

_____

_____

_____

_____

_____

5. How do you feed your dragon? _____

_____

_____

_____

_____

6. How does your dragon influence you? _____

_____

_____

7. Where do you think your dragon wants to take you? _____

_____

_____

_____

_____

8. What damage is this dragon causing to Your spouse? Your marriage? Your family? Your work?

_____

_____

_____

_____

_____

_____

Prayer

Dear God,

Help me see my dragon for what it truly is; something that I worship.

At first, it was exciting, but now it causes me grief.

Help me understand how it seeks to control me.

Show me how I can give myself completely to you, oh God.

Show me how I can worship you.

Help me see all the good things you have done for me. Help me to realize a new life in you.

So Be It! – Amen.

Week # 1

"And so, dear brothers and sisters,
I plead with you to give your bodies to God
because of all he has done for you. Let them be a living and holy
sacrifice—the kind he will find acceptable.
This is truly the way to worship him.
Don't copy the behavior and customs of this world,
but let God transform you into a new person
by changing the way you think.
Then you will learn to know God's will for you,
which is good and pleasing and perfect."

Romans 12:1-2

"Transformation is a process, and as life happens there are tons of ups and downs.
It's a journey of discovery - there are moments on mountaintops and moments in
deep valleys of despair."

Rick Warren

Transforming your old way of thinking, thinking that slays you, requires a spiritual process. New thinking changes your heart and mind towards your addiction dragon.

Some recent discoveries in Neuroplasticity in the last few decades seem to agree with the renewing principle of Romans 12:1-2. Neuroplasticity is "the brain's ability to reorganize itself by forming new neural connections throughout life." Neuroplasticity points to a "renewed mind." It's the brain's ability to restructure itself with repetitive training and practice. It's one of the most popular areas of psychology today.

Written almost two thousand years ago, Paul possessed some insight into the brain's malleable qualities when he wrote Romans 12:1-2. Simply put, with training, practice, and God's help, your brain can change how it thinks.

Redirect your worship. The word "worship" comes from an old English word meaning "worthship" or "worthiness." What you value as worthy defines your worship. You look at addiction because you value it. Addiction is a false form of worship. Value better things. Value yourself. Value your relationships. Value that valuable above your addiction.

Boundaries –

What weak boundaries hurt you? What new boundaries need establishing? What Old Boundaries need tearing down?

_____

_____

_____

_____

_____

Accountability –

Whose part of your team helping you overcome your dragon?

_____

_____

_____

_____

Who do you answer to?

_____

_____

Confession – (To agree about a thing, reveal it, or expose a secret)

Agree with God about your weaknesses, failings, and harm. Be honest. Tell it like it is. Be specific. God this week I:

_____

_____

_____

_____

Knowledge –

What did you learn about yourself this week?

_____

_____

_____

_____

Your Struggle?

_____

_____

About God?

_____

_____

About Others?

_____

_____

Sorrow –

How does God view your struggle this past week?

_____

_____

_____

What about you?

_____

_____

_____

Others?_____

_____

Thoughts?_____

_____

_____

Meditation

"God uses broken things. It takes broken soil to produce a crop, broken clouds to give rain, broken grain to give bread, broken bread to give strength. It is the broken alabaster box that gives forth perfume. It is Peter, weeping bitterly, who returns to greater power than ever."

Vance Havner

Ponder –

1. What hope do you find in the above words?

_____

_____

_____

_____

2. What corrections do you need to make?

_____

_____

_____

3. What personal thoughts spring out?

_____

_____

_____

_____

Write out a prayer today. Give it a try. Go ahead. A sincere prayer from your heart is a soul's breath.

_____

_____

_____

_____

_____

_____

_____

_____

Notes

Week # 2

*"Like a **muddied spring** or a **polluted well**
are the righteous who give way to the wicked."*

Proverbs 25:26

*"No good water comes from a muddy spring.
No sweet fruit comes from a bitter seed."*

Jose Rizal

Perhaps, no verse in the Bible sums up the reality of addiction-living better than Proverbs 25:26. Person after person muddies their lives crossing addiction's boundary to drink at poisoned, polluted waters of their well. Yes, at first, the waters are cool and refreshing. However, waters from this well create a ferocious thirst impossible to quench. The more one drinks, the more insatiable one's desires become. As one drinks its poison, it seeps into the very fabric of the person changing one's personality.

As one yields, one falls and compromises integrity. Addiction muddies a person sometimes beyond recognition. Ultimately a person doesn't recognize who he or she has become. Worse yet, a person doesn't understand the process transforming them into the person they despise.

Boundaries –

How did you pollute your wells (integrity) this week? What new boundaries need establishing? What Old Boundaries need tearing down?

_____

_____

_____

_____

_____

Accountability –

Who's helping you overcome your dragon? What accountability worked well this week? What failed? Why?

_____

_____

_____

_____

Who do you answer to?

_____

_____

Confession – (To agree about a thing, reveal it, or expose a secret)

How does your dragon sully your person, character, and integrity? Confess it to God right here:

_____

_____

_____

_____

Knowledge –

What did you learn about yourself this week?

_____

_____

_____

_____

Your Polluted Well?

_____

_____

What Mud Exists?

_____

_____

How can you clean it up?

_____

_____

Sorrow –

How does God view your encounters with your dragon this past week?

_____

_____

_____

_____

You? _____

_____

_____

Others?_____

_____

Thoughts?_____

_____

_____

Meditation

"There's no clear water from a muddy well. All you can do is let the silt settle until the water clears otherwise it will taste sour."

Patrick Roth fuss, The Wise Man's Fear."

Ponder –

What hope do you find in the above words?

_____

_____

_____

_____

What corrections do you need to make?

_____

_____

_____

Personal Thoughts:

_____

_____

_____

_____

A Prayer Today

Dear God,
Help me take my dragon seriously.
Help me see its devastating effects.
Help me see the immense damage it's causing; to myself, to those
around me, and to those enslaved by it.
Help me see the ruined lives left in its wake.
Dear God, help me start to take this thing seriously.
Change my heart, oh God. Help me see anew. Mold and make me
into the person – the mom, dad, husband, wife, son, daughter, friend that you desire me
to become.
Help me develop a plan to combat and defeat my addiction.
Give me the hope for the victory you have promised – the victory only
you can give.
                    So Be It! – Amen.

Notes

Week # 3

*"You have already **won a victory** over those people, because the Spirit **who lives in you is greater than the spirit who lives in the world**."*

1 John 4:4

"Victory has a thousand fathers, but defeat is an orphan."

John F. Kennedy

Boundaries –

What victories occurred for you this week? What boundary helped win this victory? No victories? What new boundaries needs building?

_____

_____

_____

_____

_____

Accountability –

Who did you call when tempted to fall again? Why? Why not? What accountability worked well this week? What failed? Why?

_____

_____

_____

_____

Who did you answer to?

_____

_____

Confession – (To agree about a thing, reveal it, or expose a secret)

Confess that God can help your grasp victory. Confess it to God right here:

_____

_____

_____

_____

Knowledge –

What did you learn about yourself this week?

_____

_____

_____

_____

How do you pollute your well?

_____

_____

_____

_____

What Mud Exists in your waters of life?

_____

_____

_____

_____

How can you clean it up?

_____

_____

Sorrow –

How does God view your struggle this week?

_____

_____

_____

_____

You? _____

_____

_____

Others?_____

_____

Thoughts? _____

_____

_____

Meditation

"I thank you for answering my prayer and giving me victory!"

Psalm 118:21

"For every child of God defeats this evil world, and we achieve this victory through our faith."

1 John 5:4

Ponder –

What hope do you find in the above words?

_____

_____

_____

_____

What corrections do you need to make?

_____

_____

_____

Personal Thoughts:

_____

_____

_____

_____

A Prayer Today

Dear God,
Help me take my dragon seriously.
Help me see its devastating effects.
Help me see the immense damage it's causing; to myself, to those
around me, and to those enslaved by it.
Help me see the ruined lives left in its wake.
Dear God, help me start to take this thing seriously.
Change my heart, oh God. Help me see anew. Mold and make me
into the person – the mom, dad, husband, wife, son, daughter, friend that you desire me
to become.
Help me develop a plan to combat and defeat this evilness.
Give me the hope for the victory you have promised – the victory only
you can give.

So Be It! – Amen.

Week # 4

*"Stand fast therefore in the liberty by which **Christ has made us free**, and **do not be entangled** again with a yoke of bondage."*

Gal 5:1 (NKJV)

"Addiction isn't about substance - you aren't addicted to the substance, you are addicted to the alteration of mood that the substance brings."

Susan Cheever

Boundaries –

What victories occurred for you this week? What boundary helped establish this victory? What Old Boundaries need tearing down? What new boundary needs building?

_____

_____

_____

_____

_____

Accountability –

Who did you call when tempted to fall again? Why? Why not? What accountability worked well this week? What failed?

_____

_____

_____

_____

Who did you answer to?

_____

_____

Confession – (To agree about a thing, reveal it, or expose a secret)

Tell God about your dragon. Be specific. How are you responsible for the habit that troubles you?

_____

_____

_____

_____

Knowledge –

What bondage does your dragon cause you?

_____

_____

_____

_____

How does your dragon entangle your life?

_____

_____

_____

_____

Describe your dragon.

_____

_____

_____

_____

Sorrow –

How does God view your struggle this week?

_____

_____

_____

_____

You? _____

_____

_____

Others? _____

_____

Thoughts? _____

_____

_____

Meditation

*"Our past may explain why we're suffering
but we must not use it as an excuse to stay in <u>bondage</u>."*

Joyce Meyer, Battlefield of the Mind: Winning the Battle in Your Mind

Ponder –

What hope do you find in the above words?

_____

_____

_____

_____

What changes do you need to make?

_____

_____

_____

Any Personal Thoughts?

_____

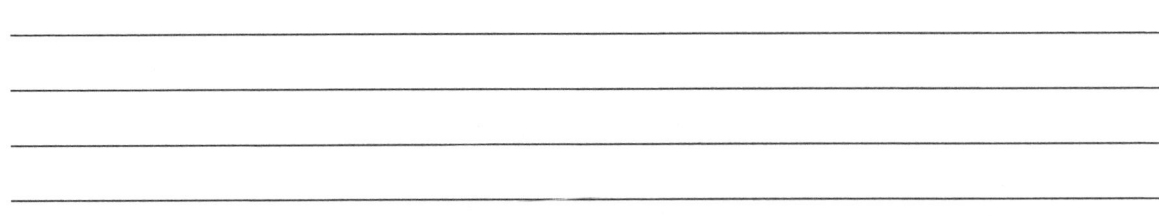

A Prayer Today

Dear God,

Help me see the bondage my habit brings not only to me but all those around me.

Help me understand, oh God, what this life of slavery brings. Not only to me, but to my spouse, my family, friends, church, and community.

Show me freedom in your Son Jesus Christ.

This is the wonderful relationship you offer me.

Help me seize this opportunity. Take away the damaged guilty feelings of my heart.

Those feelings telling me I am helpless, worthless, and alone.

Help me see your goodness, your forgiveness, and, my next steps with you.

So Be It – Amen.

Notes – Perhaps Your Own Prayer?

Week # 5

*"I **discipline** my body like an athlete, training it to do what it should.*
Otherwise, I fear that after preaching to others
*I myself might be **disqualified**."*

1 Corinthians 9:27

"Lay Your back into it!"

The Pirate Primer: Mastering the Language of Swashbucklers and Rogues
by George Choundas

Boundaries –

What discipline is required to build healthy boundaries in your life?

_____

_____

_____

_____

_____

Accountability –

Who did you call when your dragon temped you? Who can help you train to master your shortcomings?

_____

_____

_____

_____

Who do you answer to? Just to yourself? How's that working for you?

_____

_____

Confession – (To agree about a thing, reveal it, or expose a secret)

Tell God about your lack of discipline. Be specific. How are you responsible for empowering your dragon? How might you train yourself to gain strength over your dragon?

_____

_____

_____

_____

Knowledge –

What bondage does your dragon cause you?

_____

_____

_____

_____

How does your dragon pollute your life?

_____

_____

Describe your dragon's ways of tempting you.

_____

_____

_____

_____

_____

Sorrow –

How does God view your dragon?

_____

_____

_____

_____

You? _____

_____

_____

Others?_____

_____

Thoughts?_____

_____

_____

Meditation

"Discipline imposed from the outside eventually defeats
when it is not matched by desire from within."

Dawson Trotman

Ponder –

What is your action plan to manage your addiction?

_____

_____

_____

_____

_____

_____

What is your Discipline and Desire? How does your desire on the inside match your discipline?

_____

_____

_____

_____

_____

Any Personal Thoughts?

_____

_____

_____

_____

_____

A Prayer Today

"Oh God, repeatedly, I've given myself to this habit.
Continually I fail and fall.
What once seemed my friend is now an evil enemy seeking to destroy me, destroy my
family, destroy my future, and destroy my soul.
God, I need your help. I need your strength. I need you.
I need to be made over again. I need to be renewed. Apart from you
I will continue to fail over and over again.
Without you, I am defeated.
Without you I am nothing. I am losing this fight.
So, I look to you, oh God, to you and you only.
Be my High Tower, oh God.
Be my Refuge and my Strength.
Save me, God, by your tender love and mercies. I look only to you for
strength and deliverance.
Please help me give myself to you always.
                              So be it – Amen.

Week # 6

"Be strong in the Lord and in his mighty power.
Put on all of God's armor so that you will be able
*to **stand firm against all strategies of the devil**.*
For we are not fighting against flesh-and-blood enemies,
but against evil rulers and authorities of the unseen world, against
mighty powers in this dark world,
and against evil spirits in the heavenly places."

Ephesians 6:10-12

"When the storms of life come, if they come to me personally, to my family or to the
world, I want to be strong enough to stand and be a strength to somebody else, be
shelter for somebody else."

Anne Graham Lotz

Ask any successful athlete about the immense suffering they put their bodies through to compete successfully. I've known several people in South Africa who ran the Comrades Marathon. This marathon, run every year the end of May, is the oldest ultramarathon in the world. The course is more than 56 miles. Almost unbelievable, isn't it?

Competitors pound out thousands of miles running to prepare for this one marathon. They deny themselves sweets, fatty foods, and alcohol. They train through injuries and sickness. They sacrifice recreational time with family and friends. They train, train, and then train some more! Then the day of the race comes. Waking up early, 11,000 people stand ready at the starting line. The pistol fires and they are off and running.

Eleven grueling hours are allotted to complete this race. World-class runners finish in under six hours. And what do they receive for all their troubles as they cross the finish line? A small, rather worthless medal is all they carry home after their race. That, and a lot of stiffness, soreness, and pain! I knew several runners, after finishing the Comrades Marathon, their toenails turned black and fell off! Yet, every person I've talked with among those who finished the race maintained it was well worth it! Just to finish was more than enough reward!

That approach to training—to finish—is the idea you need to understand in 1 Corinthians 9:27. I "discipline my body," he writes, using the Greek word, hypoppiazo, which literally means to beat yourself black and blue. Paul perhaps meant this quite literally. It was a word used in the day for a boxer or athlete handling his body roughly to prepare for competition in athletic events.

Boundaries –

Where are you falling in your battle against your dragon?

_____

_____

_____

_____

_____

Accountability –

How can you "subdue" your body? Bring it into submission. Discipline it. Who can help you?

_____

_____

_____

_____

Who do you answer to? Just to yourself? How's that working for you?

_____

_____

_____

Confession – (To agree about a thing, reveal it, or expose a secret)

How do you give into your dragon? Tell it to God. Be specific.

_____

_____

_____

_____

Knowledge –

What is needed to stand strong? How can you train?

_____

_____

_____

_____

How does your dragon gain power over your life?

_____

_____

_____

_____

_____

Talk about how you can depower your dragon. Starve your dragon's will.

_____

_____

_____

_____

_____

Sorrow –

How can God become your strength?

_____

_____

_____

_____

Describe the sorrow your dragon causes you.

_____

_____

_____

What about God's sorrow seeing you suffer with your dragon?

_____

_____

Thoughts? _____

_____

_____

Meditation

But I keep praying to you, Lord, hoping this time you will show me favor.
  In your unfailing love, O God, answer my prayer with your sure salvation.
Rescue me from the mud; don't let me sink any deeper!
  Save me from those who hate me, and pull me from these deep waters.
Don't let the floods overwhelm me, or the deep waters swallow me,
  or the pit of death devour me.
Answer my prayers, O Lord, for your unfailing love is wonderful.
  Take care of me, for your mercy is so plentiful.

Psalm 69:13-16

Ponder –

What does your action plan to defeat your addiction look like?

_____

_____

_____

_____

What hope? _____

_____

_____

What are your thoughts about "unfailing" love?

_____

_____

_____

How'd your action plan go this week? Any success? Failure?

_____

_____

_____

_____

_____

Write Your Own Prayer Again This Week – Work on it – You can do it!

_____

_____

_____

_____

_____

_____

_____

_____

_____

_____

Week # 7

*"But among you there must not be even **a hint of sexual immorality**, or of any kind of **impurity**, or of **greed**, because these are improper for God's holy people."*

Ephesians 5:3

"Soft addictions are an alluring, seductive aspect of our culture - they are easy to attain and socially acceptable, they are even encouraged in many cases. Yet they are lethal to the spirit."

Judith Wright

"What lies behind us and what lies before us are tiny matters compared to what lies within us."

— Ralph Waldo Emerson

Boundaries –

What hints of the dragon exists in your lifestyle? Movies that you watch? Music you listen to? Conversations? Social Media? Associations, Places, Settings?

_____

_____

_____

_____

_____

Accountability –

Who can hold your hand to the fire to help you live above your dragon?

_____

_____

_____

_____

Who did you answer to this week? Just to yourself? Again, how's that working for you?

_____

_____

Confession – (To agree about a thing, reveal it, or expose a secret)

When did you give into your dragon? Tell God. Be specific. This week ,how did you soil yourself with that which is not pure and whole to your person?

_____

_____

_____

_____

_____

_____

Knowledge –

What is needed to stand strong? What does your training look like to defeat your dragon?

_____

_____

_____

_____

How does your dragon offer you a sense of false satisfaction?

_____

_____

_____

_____

_____

Describe your dragon. What does it look like? What does it feel like? Where does it take you?

_____

_____

_____

_____

_____

Sorrow –

Where does your dragon leave you at the end?

_____

_____

_____

_____

How can God help you?

_____

_____

_____

How can you help yourself?

_____

_____

_____

What about God's sorrow, seeing you bring yourself into so much suffering?

_____

_____

Thoughts? _____

_____

_____

Meditation

"Let your unfailing love surround us, LORD, for our hope is in you alone."

Psalm 33:22

*"Your unfailing love, O LORD, is as vast as the heavens;
your faithfulness reaches beyond the clouds.*

*"Your righteousness is like the mighty mountains, your justice like the ocean depths.
You care for people and animals alike, O LORD."*

*"How precious is your unfailing love, O God!
All humanity finds shelter in the shadow of your wings."*

Psalm 36:5-7

Ponder –

What ENCOURAGEMENT do you find in the above words?

_____

_____

_____

_____

What HOPE exists for you here?

_____

_____

What are your thoughts about "unfailing" love?

_____

_____

_____

Any Personal Thoughts?

_____

_____

_____

_____

_____

Write Your Own Prayer Again This Week – Work on it – You can do it!

Week # 8

"If your right eye makes you stumble and leads you to sin, tear it out and throw it away [that is, remove yourself from the source of temptation]; for it is better for you to lose one of the parts of your body, than for your whole body to be thrown into hell."

Matthew 5:29 (AMP)

"Start by doing what's necessary; then do what's possible; and suddenly you are doing the impossible."

Francis of Assisi

"The only person you are destined to become is the person you decide to be."

– Ralph Waldo Emerson

Boundaries –

What boundary do you need to fortify to help you plug the holes in your defenses? What harmful boundaries did you cross over this week? Work on it. Build your walls. Think it through.

_____

_____

_____

_____

_____

_____

Accountability –

Who can you rally around you that will help you build impenetrable personal defenses?

_____

_____

_____

_____

Who DID you answer to THIS WEEK? Yourself? No one? How's that working for you?

_____

_____

_____

Confession – (To agree about a thing, reveal it, or expose a secret)

How did you give into your dragon this week? Tell it to God. Be specific.

_____

_____

_____

_____

Knowledge –

What is needed to keep you from offending yourself? Remember Jesus words in Matthew 5:29.

_____

_____

_____

_____

What can you do to weaken your dragon's power in your life?

_____

_____

Describe what it might take to accomplish this.

_____

_____

_____

_____

_____

Sorrow –

What sorrow did you experience this week because of your dragon? What sorrow did others experience? What do you think God's sorrow is watching you hurt yourself?

_____

_____

_____

_____

_____

_____

Describe the sorrow your dragon causes you?

_____

_____

_____

How do you think God views your struggles?

_____

_____

Thoughts? _____

_____

_____

Meditation

"A dream doesn't become reality through magic;
it takes sweat, determination and hard work."

Colin Powell

Ponder –

What challenge do you find in the above words?

_____

_____

_____

_____

Describe your determination. How does your dream match your determination?

_____

_____

_____

Personal Thoughts

_____

_____

_____

_____

_____

Prayer

Dear God,
Help me see the bondage my dragon brings not only to me but all those around me.
Help me understand, oh God, what this life of slavery brings.
Not only to me, but to my spouse, my family, friends, church, and community.
Show the freedom you offer me.
The wonderful relationship you offer me.
Help me seize this opportunity.
Take away the damaged guilty feelings of my heart.
Those feelings telling me I am helpless, worthless, and alone.
Help me see your goodness, your forgiveness, and, my next steps with you.

So Be It – Amen.

Week # 9

*"As iron **sharpens** iron,*
*So one man **sharpens** [and **influences**]*
another [through discussion]."

Proverbs 27:17 (AMP)

"In the pain, the agony, and the heroic endeavors of life, we pass through a refiner's fire, and the insignificant and the unimportant in our lives can melt away like dross and make our faith bright, intact, and strong."

James E. Faust

"Our greatest glory is not in never failing, but in rising up every time we fail."

– Ralph Waldo Emerson

Boundaries –

How are your boundaries sharpening your defenses to protect you from that which slays you?

_____

_____

_____

_____

_____

Accountability –

Who is sharpening you through honest accurate discussions about your dragon? How?

_____

_____

_____

_____

How might your accountability be more like being part of a team rather than just answering for your failures?

_____

_____

_____

Confession – (To agree about a thing, reveal it, or expose a secret)

How did you change God's image of you this week into something less, unfulfilling, and unsatisfying?

_____

_____

_____

_____

Knowledge –

Write down all you know about your dragon. What's does the dragon cost you?

_____

_____

_____

_____

_____

What is one principle from your above discovery you can apply to your life this week?

_____

_____

Describe what it might take to accomplish this.

_____

_____

_____

_____

_____

Sorrow –

How do you think God grieves for you when you fall into a destructive habit, thought, or reaction?

_____

_____

_____

_____

Describe your sorrow about your dragon? Look at 2 Corinthians 7:10 in the Bible.

_____

_____

_____

How do you think God feels about all this stuff?

_____

_____

Thoughts? _____

_____

_____

Meditation

***"If you hear a voice within you say 'you cannot paint,'
then by all means paint and that voice will be silenced."***

Vincent Van Gogh

Ponder –

What are your inner voices saying to you write now?

_____

_____

_____

_____

What can you do to silence negative self-talk within you? Where's a more positive soul-voice?

_____

_____

_____

Personal Thoughts

_____

_____

_____

_____

_____

Prayer – Renew Your Mind

Dear God,
Yes, I need a good accountability partner to help me deal with my dragons.
Please help me find the right person living above this problem,
A person who will hold me accountable in this battle.
A person who asks the tough questions, and provides the right answers.
Help me find that person who will speak truth to me.
A person I can call on in my times of temptation and trouble.
Most of all help me become the person who will take responsibility for
my own change. Help me learn to honor you in all I do.

So Be It! – Amen.

Week # 10

*"**Guard your heart** above all else,*
*for **it determines the course** of your life."*

Proverbs 4:23

"The happiness of your life depends upon the quality of your thoughts: therefore, guard accordingly, and take care that you entertain no notions unsuitable to virtue and reasonable nature."

Marcus Aurelius

"All the suffering, stress, and addiction comes from not realizing you already are what you are looking for."

Jon Kabat-Zinn

The Great Wall of China is one of the great marvels of the ancient world. Built over 15 centuries through numerous dynasties it spanned over 4,000 miles. The first boundary was constructed by Shi Huang, the first emperor of China who lived between 259 and 210 BC. In the early stages, it served as a barrier to protect one clan from another. Over the centuries, as China's dominance grew, better, stronger, and higher walls were constructed to protect China from her enemies, particularly in the North. As massively impressive as the walls were, enemies breached the walls repeatedly. Armies either went around them, flanking the furthest extents of the walls, or they penetrated the weakest sections. Often, they entered through the portals of the wall, that is, the gates themselves.

In AD 1644, the Manchus broke through the Great Wall and overran China. They did this by bribing a Chinese general of the Ming dynasty to open the gates. The impressively fortified structure built to keep enemies from gaining access failed. The wall, built over 12 centuries and requiring the labor of more than 1,000,000 people, it turned out, could not withstand the enemy from within. The greatest enemy was not outside the wall. That enemy lived within them.

Boundaries –

What boundaries guard your heart? How strong are your boundaries? How can you strengthen your boundaries? Think about it. Work on it. Where are you defenses strong? Where are they weak?

_____

_____

_____

_____

_____

Accountability –

Who is helping you guard your heart? How? What else must you do to build a stronger team?

_____

_____

_____

_____

How is your accountability like being part of a team rather than just answering for your dragon?

_____

_____

_____

Confession – (To agree about a thing, reveal it, or expose a secret)

Confess your failures to guard your wonderful heart-soul. Confess the sins others committed against you that wounded your heart. Look carefully at 1 John 1:9 in the Bible. "Cleanses us from ALL our sins."

_____

_____

_____

_____

Knowledge –

What would it take to guard your heart? What new action must you take?

_____

_____

_____

_____

_____

_____

_____

_____

_____

_____

_____

Sorrow –

How do you think God grieves for you when you give into to your dragon?

_____

_____

_____

_____

Describe your sorrow about your dragon? Look at 2 Corinthians 7:10 again in the Bible.

_____

_____

_____

How do you think God feels about all this stuff?

_____

_____

Thoughts? _____

_____

_____

Meditation

"We are not responsible for what breaks us,
but we can be responsible for what puts us back together again.
Naming the hurt is how we begin to repair our broken parts."

Bishop Desmond Tutu
The Book of Forgiving: The Fourfold Path for Healing Ourselves and Our World

Ponder –

What hurts hides behind your dragon? This part is tough.

_____

_____

_____

_____

_____

_____

_____

_____

_____

_____

Who do you need to ask forgiveness? To whom do you need to offer forgiveness?

_____

_____

_____

Personal Thoughts

_____

_____

_____

_____

_____

Prayer This Week – Pray it every day.

God,
I must begin to take my dragon habit seriously.
Help me to see the damaging nature of my bondage.
Help me see what it's doing to my life.
Help me understand the negative effects that oppress my family.
Show the path to true relationships outside my current thinking.
Show me protections I can use to close off access to this habit.
Show me where I need to change. Give me the strength to make those changes.
Give me the tenacity to stick with those changes.
Give me someone who will hold me to my changes.
There are so, so many temptations. Help me remove the rubble and close the holes as well as I can.

So Be It – Amen.

Week # 11

"Dear brothers and sisters, if another believer is overcome by some sin,
you who are godly should gently and humbly help
that person back onto the right path.
And be careful not to fall into the same temptation yourself.
Share each other's burdens, *and in this way obey the law of Christ."*

Galatians 6:1-2

"It is not from your own goods that you give to the beggar; it is a portion of his own
that you are restoring to him. The Earth belongs to all. So, you are paying back a
debt and think you are making a gift to which you are not bound."

Saint Ambrose

Boundaries –

What boundaries helped you get back on the right track? What weak boundaries need strengthening or elimination? Strengthen your walls!

_____

_____

_____

_____

_____

Accountability –

Who is helping you back onto the right path? How? When? Where?

_____

_____

_____

_____

Write about your accountability team. Friends, family, church, recovery groups, resources, etc.

_____

_____

_____

_____

_____

_____

_____

_____

Confession – (To agree about a thing, reveal it, or expose a secret)

Reveal your faults. Open a little more about them. Come on. You can do this. Take ownership.

_____

_____

_____

_____

_____

Knowledge –

What temptations presented themselves in the face of your dragon?

_____

_____

_____

_____

_____

_____

_____

_____

_____

_____

_____

Sorrow –

How do you think God grieves for you when you fall to your dragon?

_____

_____

_____

_____

Describe the sorrow about your dragon? Look at 2 Corinthians 7:10 in the Bible again. Think about this verse a bit.

_____

_____

_____

How do you think God feels about all this stuff? How do you feel about it? What's in your soul?

_____

_____

Meditation

Have you been faithful to God today?

Have you been faithful to your spouse?

Have you been faithful to your family?

Have you been faithful to yourself?

Ponder –

"Faithful" – Any thoughts?

_____

_____

_____

_____

_____

_____

_____

_____

_____

_____

_____

Who do you need to ask forgiveness? To whom do you need to offer forgiveness?

_____

_____

_____

Personal Thoughts

_____

_____

_____

_____

_____

Prayer:

> *Dear God,*
> *Yes, I need a good accountability partner to help me deal with my dragon.*
> *Please help me find the right person living above this problem,*
> *A person who will hold me accountable in this battle.*
> *A person who asks the tough questions, and provides the right answers.*
> *Help me find that person who speaks truth to me.*
> *Help me find this person soon.*
> *A person, group, or confidant I can call on in my times of temptation and trouble.*
> *Most of all help me become the person who will take responsibility for*
> *my own change. Help me learn to honor you in all I do.*
>
> *So Be It! – Amen.*

Week # 12

*"People who **conceal** their sins (dragon) will not prosper, but it they **confess** and turn from them, they will **receive mercy**."*

Proverbs 28:13
Parenthesis Mine

"Either we finish them, or they'll finish us! It's the only way we'll be rid of them! If we find the nest and destroy it, the dragons will leave."

How to Train Your Dragon

While trying to assist a young man struggling with an addiction, I listened as he confessed, "Dear God, I'm sorry for doing this again. I know it's not a good thing. Help me to do better. Amen." I looked straight into his eyes and said, "Is this perhaps one reason you're not getting victory over this in your life right now? Is this how you confess your addiction to your spouse, family, and friends?" "What do you mean?" he shot back.

I said, "That's really not a confession. It's pretty weak. If you really want to be rid of this thing, the secret is in confession. Confession must be patterned after the Bible. Can I show you what confession really looks like?" With that, we began.

King David, the second king of ancient Israel and author of many of the Psalms, wrote Psalms 32 and 51. The Book of Psalms is a collection of lyric poems, originally set to music, and each is a prayer, thought, or meditation. Psalms 32 and 51 are part of a collection of seven repentance Psalms. We believe King David wrote these two Psalms after committing horrible atrocities that sprang from sexual addiction. King David became a very proficient confessor. He needed to. Read Psalms 32 & 51. Meditate upon them. Think about them. Grasp hold of their truths. See what it feels like to experience complete forgiveness and release!

Boundaries –

How do your boundaries reveal your Dragon's presence? How do they defend yourself against your dragon? How are your boundaries failing? How did your boundaries fail this past week?

_____

_____

_____

_____

_____

Accountability –

Name your team members this week who held you accountable. Place? Time? Resources?

_____

_____

_____

_____

Write about one good thing on your accountability team offers you.

_____

_____

_____

Confession – (To agree about a thing, reveal it, or expose a secret)

Reveal your faults. Open a little more about them. Come on. You can do this. Open. Open. Open.

_____

_____

_____

_____

_____

Knowledge –

What temptations presented themselves in the face of your dragon this past week? How does your dragon gain control over you?

_____

_____

_____

_____

_____

_____

_____

_____

_____

_____

Sorrow –

How do you think God cries for you when you fall to a destructive habit, thought, or reaction?

_____

_____

_____

_____

Describe your sorrow about your dragon? Look at 2 Corinthians 7:10 in the Bible again. Think about this verse a bit more.

_____

_____

_____

How do you think God feels about all this stuff? How do you feel about it? What's in your soul?

_____

_____

Meditation

"For you are my hiding place; you protect me from trouble.
You surround me with songs of victory."

Psalm 32:7

"The LORD is a shelter for the oppressed, a refuge in times of trouble."

Psalm 9:9

"Those who live in the shelter of the Most High will find rest in the shadow of the Almighty."

Isaiah 91:1

Ponder –

_____

_____

_____

_____

_____

_____

_____

_____

_____

_____

_____

_____

Who do you need to ask forgiveness? To whom do you need to offer forgiveness?

_____

_____

_____

Personal Thoughts

_____

_____

_____

_____

_____

Prayer:

Dear God,
I'm back again struggling with this dragon thing.
I've given into my dragon repeatedly.
Help me hold myself to account of this.
Please help me gain strength over this problem.
Hold my hand as I walk through this.
Help me see the person you created me to be,
The person you want me to become,
The image you wish me to return.
Let me see me, the way you see me, as the person I can become. The person you love.
Most of all help me become the person who will take responsibility for
my own change. Help me learn to honor you in all I do.

So Be It! – Amen.

Week # 13

*"Finally, I confessed [opened, took ownership of my actions, clearly named] all my sins [dragons] to you and **stopped trying to hide my guilt**. I said to myself, 'I will confess my rebellion to the LORD.' **And you forgave me! All my guilt is gone**."*

Psalm 32:5
Brackets Mine

"I have absolutely no pleasure in the stimulants in which I sometimes so madly indulge. It has not been in the pursuit of pleasure that I have periled life and reputation and reason. It has been the desperate attempt to escape from torturing memories, from a sense of insupportable loneliness and a dread of some strange impending doom."

Edgar Allan Poe

"Confession of errors is like a broom which sweeps away the dirt and leaves the surface brighter and clearer. I feel stronger for confession."

Mahatma Gandhi

To Confess or Not to Confess

Among people dealing with addiction, confession is pathetically weak or nonexistent. It's not that these struggling people's lives are prayerless. Oh, they pray! They beg for help and mercy all the time. They just rarely confess the depth and depravity of their addictions and their affect upon those around them. Let alone confess their self-centered worship to a heavenly God. Often, in embarrassment, they fear to acknowledge their deeds to themselves, family, friends, and God.

Confessionless living has negative consequences on a person's health. King David in Psalms 32 and 51 talked about "wasting away" and "groaning" all day long. The idea is literally that of growing old before one's time or to be completely used up. This certainly describes many long-time addiction sufferers.

Unconfessed sin will eat you alive, bringing about undesirable side effects. Perhaps the worst consequence of unconfessed sin is you'll not realize the process of degradation taking place within you and around you.

Then, David described God's heavy hand of discipline upon him. In Psalm 51, he said that he was broken. God's discipline of His people sets a recurring theme throughout the entire Bible. Simply put, if you belong to God, He cares about you. He disciplines those He loves. He reserves the right as Creator to discipline you as heavily and severely as needed to get you back on track; His track. Many your current streak of bad luck is really a lovely God trying to bring you back online.

Scripture teaches God disciplines those He truly loves. If you are under the heavy hand of God's discipline, it's because He's trying to bring you to the point of confession. **Maybe all the cruddy stuff in your life right now is God trying to bring you to a healthier place?**

David described God's discipline upon him as harsh. It literally sapped his strength. He lamented, "My strength evaporated like water in the summer heat …" The image is a person fainting from sunstroke. In David's unconfessed state, he fainted in the heat of God's discipline upon his life.

Next, the mental and emotional turmoil of living in such a state became unbearable. In this David said, "For I recognize my rebellion; it haunts me day and night." David lived as a haunted man trying to hide his secret life. Often addicts describe their lives in terms of nightmares. One desperately cried, **"It's like my life is a <u>haunted</u> <u>house</u>. Everywhere I turn, stuff keeps popping up."**

Boundaries –

What boundaries help you get back on the right track? What weak boundaries need strengthening or elimination?

_____

_____

_____

_____

_____

Accountability –

Who is helping you back onto the right path? How do you show your gratitude to them?

_____

_____

_____

_____

Write about your accountability team? Friends, family, church, recovery groups, resources, etc.

_____

_____

_____

Confession – (To agree about a thing, reveal it, or expose a secret)

What are you trying to hide about your dragon? Where's your haunted house? With yourself and God clearly describe that which trips you up repeatedly.

_____

_____

_____

_____

_____

_____

_____

_____

Knowledge –

How much do you understand about your dragon, and the path its leading you down?

_____

_____

_____

_____

_____

_____

_____

_____

_____

_____

_____

Sorrow –

What tears did your dragon cause you this week?

_____

_____

_____

What tears did your dragon cause God this past week?

_____

Meditation

"I used you, manipulated you, lied to you and broke your heart. While you cried a thousand tears for me, I was out getting high. I make no excuses. I was driven by an evil, urgent need that had no conscience, integrity, values or morals. I put you through hell and I regret that. Going forward I will stop making promises, and start making amends. In other words, I won't tell you I'm sorry, I'll show you."

May 10th, 2016 | By Lorelie Rozzano | Posted in Blog

Confessions Of An Addict (In Recovery)

http://www.addictioncampuses.com/resources/addiction-campuses-blog/confessions-of-an-addict-in-recovery/

"Confession of sin should be <u>explicit</u>... When, in the course of the day's engagements, our conscience witnesses against us that we have sinned, we should at once confess our guilt..."

David M'Intyre
The Hidden Life of Prayer.

Ponder –

How explicit are you about your confessing your dragon-addictions? Any thoughts about "our conscience of witnesses?" Who are the witnesses to your conscience?

_____

_____

_____

_____

_____

_____

_____

_____

How can you confess your fallings to your dragon?

_____

_____

_____

_____

Personal Thoughts

_____

_____

_____

_____

_____

Prayer:

God,
I confess that my dragon taints people created in your image.
My dragon violates your nature and your creation.
The dragon lies.
It's not beautiful.
It's not safe.
It's not harmless.
It's not okay.
You are a caring loving God.
You created us, me, to resemble who You are.
The dragon sullies this image.
When I sin, it violates your very nature. It harms your creation.
I confess this sin to you.
It is against you that I have sinned. God forgive me for the harm I
either knowingly or unknowingly caused to others. And, forgive me for
what I've done to myself, your creation.
Show me your mercy.
Create a clean heart in me.
Give me a right spirit.
Restore to me the joy of seeing other people as you created them.
Lead me in your way.

So Be It! – Amen.

Week # 14

*"If we acknowledge our sins, then, since he is trustworthy and just, he will forgive them and **purify** us from **all wrongdoing**."*

1 John 1:9 (CJB)

*"People who **conceal** their sins [dragons] will not prosper, but it they **confess and turn away** from them, they will **receive mercy**."*

Proverbs 28:13
Brackets Mine

We'Re The Monsters - Poem by Victoria Foister

There's a monster hiding
in the mirror

when I lean in closer
he comes nearer

he looks deep into my eyes
and sees the fear inside me

'hush baby hush' he whispers
'you're the only one who knows I'm here'.

Now. Look. In. Your. Mirror.
Your the only one who sees.

Taking a long, sobering look at the multiple layers of harm addiction causes is crucial. Understanding exactly what you do every time addiction is accessed uncovers its consequences. Know this. You never win against addiction while living in your addiction. There is never a good outcome if you and your addiction are cohorts.

Boundaries –

Who in your past, crossed your boundaries and wounded you? How might your past woundings, hurts, and injuries have exposed you to your dragons today?

_____

_____

_____

_____

_____

_____

_____

_____

Accountability –

How is accountability going? How is it helping? What needs to improve? Change of direction?

_____

_____

_____

Who are you talking with about your dragon? How does that person become a helper or enabler?

_____

_____

_____

_____

_____

_____

_____

Confession – (To agree about a thing, reveal it, or expose a secret)

Look again at 1 John 1:9 in the Bible. **"He cleanses us from <u>all</u> sin."** God can cleanse you from all your dragon's power. Even if that dragon was the result of another's sin against you. Any thoughts here? Think about this for a moment.

_____

_____

_____

_____

_____

_____

_____

_____

Knowledge –

Look back. Who or what situation introduced you to your dragon? Was it the result of someone wounding or victimizing you?

_____

_____

_____

_____

_____

_____

_____

_____

_____

_____

Sorrow –

What greatest sorrow did another cause you? When was this?

_____

_____

_____

_____

_____

_____

_____

_____

Meditation

"If God can cleanse you of your sins personally committed by you, then he can also cleanse you from the sins others perpetrated and committed against you. Being cleansed from the unrighteousness of others is often a beginning step in recovery."

Don Mingo

Ponder –

How can you confess sin, wounding, offense, or abuse of another to God and yourself? Try it. I know it's perhaps painful. Yet, confessing all sin, not yours only, but others upon your person is essential in healing and recovery.

_____

_____

_____

_____

_____
_____
_____
_____
_____
_____

Personal Thoughts

_____
_____
_____
_____
_____

Prayer:

God,
I confess that this person _____ tainted the image you created of me.
This person my _____ hurt me. Wounded me. And, damaged me.
That act feeds my dragon's hold over me, your creation.
That person and those acts are always with me.
It's not okay.
It wounded me, holding me captive to their acts against my will.
I confess these acts, their acts, and those people to you.
Free me from their sins' power over me.
You are a caring, loving God, who created me to resemble YOU.
Show me your mercy.
Wash me from their sins.
Release me from the bondage of their acts that still hold power over me.
Create a clean heart in me.
Give me a right spirit
Cleanse me from all my sin and their sin too.
Restore to me the joy of seeing other people as you created them.
Lead me in your way.

So Be It! – Amen.

Week # 15

*"For **wisdom** will come into your heart,*
and knowledge will be pleasant to you soul."

Proverbs 2:10

*"Intelligent people are always **ready to learn**.*
*Their ears are open for **knowledge**."*

Proverbs 18:15

"What fascinates me about addiction and obsessive behavior is that people would choose an altered state of consciousness that's toxic and ostensibly destroys most aspects of your normal life, because for a brief moment you feel okay."

Moby

Boundaries –

For many weeks you've worked on your boundaries. How are they more secure now? What still needs strengthening? Come on! Be honest! What step do you still need to take to move forward?

_____

_____

_____

_____

_____

_____

_____

_____

Accountability –

How does your accountability team/partner live above the control of your dragon?

_____

_____

_____

How can you strengthen your accountability team? No one said this would be easy.

_____

_____

_____

_____

_____

_____

_____

Confession – (To agree about a thing, reveal it, or expose a secret)

Look your dragon in the eye, and confess all that you see, feel, and fear to God, yourself, and others.

_____

_____

_____

_____

_____

_____

_____

_____

Knowledge –

What is the end of your road if you keep following your dragon?

_____

_____

_____

What is your dragon doing to you and to others around you?

_____

_____

_____

What more do you know about your dragon now than you did a month ago?

_____

_____

_____

_____

_____

Sorrow –

Joy comes in the morning? What does your soul's sunrise look like in your horizon? Any hope yet?

_____

_____

_____

_____

_____

_____

_____

_____

Meditation

"Any fool can know. The point is to understand."
Albert Einstein

"I cannot teach anybody anything. I can only make them think"
Socrates

"Knowledge is love and light and vision."
Helen Keller

Ponder –

What knowledge about your dragon has helped you deal with its negative effects?

_____

_____

_____

_____

_____

_____

_____

What understanding do you possess now to better help you deal with your dragon?

_____

_____

_____

_____

_____

Prayer:

> *My dragon defiles me and abuses others.*
> *God forgive me.*
> *Help me understand the suffering caused by personally empowering my dragon.*
> *Help me see the suffering I cause every time I open myself to my dragon.*
> *Help me understand and know a better way to live.*
> *Show me the end of my current path if I continue.*
> *Give me the strength and understanding to defeat my dragon's appeal and power.*
> *Oh, God, forgive me.*
> *Make this sink into my heart.*
> *Change my heart, oh, God.*
> *Make me more like You.*
> *Cleanse me from my wicked ways.*
> *Help me love people more than I love myself.*
> *Let me see the end of my current habits.*
> *Lead me in the way of everlasting life.*
>
> *So Be It! – Amen.*

Week # 16

*"For the kind of **sorrow** God wants us to experience **leads us away** from sin and results in salvation. There is no regret for that kind of sorrow. But **worldly sorrow**, which lacks repentance, **results in spiritual death**."*

2 Corinthians 7:10

*"Any mind that is capable of real **sorrow** is capable of good."*

Harriet Beecher Stowe

*"I hate her." Merlin laughed, tossing the stick down. "Not so. You have forgotten how to love. That's a different **sorrow**."*

Catherine Fisher

Many struggling with addiction dwell only in the second "sorrow" of 2 Corinthians 7:10; **worldly sorrow**. This is the only sorrow this world offers. This sorrow, produces death. This sorrow is marked by guilt, self-loathing, self-hate, sadness, withdrawal, isolation, unhappiness, and death. Every addiction who has ever spoken with me about their addiction suffers this guilt. As one guy in his mid-30s put it, "I always feel like such a big piece of crap after coming home drunk." A woman shared, "Look at me. My looks are ruined from doing all this meth. I hate myself."

God's Sorrow, however, is grounded in love, correction, discipline, and integrity. People feel badly about their addictive actions. They bear huge amounts of remorse and regret. Here's the thing. You feel guilty because to some degree you are guilty. We all are. When one gets caught, sorrow exponentially increases as the consequences for actions appear. Just feeling bad isn't enough, however. God doesn't delight in your living in guilt, remorse, self-loathing, and defeat.

Worldly sorrow is not God's intention. This sorrow leads to just feeling bad—period. It's a horrible place to live. Living here produces often miserable beings. It's a destructive sorrow. "A sorrow of this world" or "worldly sorrow" is a self-condemning, self-defacing, self-accusing, self-defeating, and self-returning sorrow. Since its focus is on self, it always returns to self. Self alone fails to overcome addiction. In worldly sorrow, I see people who absolutely hate themselves. In hating yourself, you can't win. Not here. Not at this point. You must move to another place, a better place. Yes, a good sorrow exists! It's there for your grasping and healing. Healing-Sorrow is God's intention for your deliverance and restoration.

Boundaries –

How are your boundaries leading you away from your dragon and towards better living?

_____

_____

_____

_____

_____

_____

_____

_____

Accountability –

How did your accountability team/partner help lead you away from your dragon this week?

_____

_____

_____

What else needs to be done?

_____

_____

_____

_____

_____

Confession – (To agree about a thing, reveal it, or expose a secret)

How sorrowful are you about giving time to your dragon? Sorrowful enough to turn away forever? How about this week? What about today? How about this moment. Right now?

_____

_____

_____

Knowledge –

Talk about these two types of sorrow at bit.

Godly sorrow – How God sees you suffering right here. Right now.

_____

_____

_____

_____

Worldly sorrow – How you see your suffering.

_____

_____

_____

_____

How can godly sorrow help your personally depower your dragon? See it the way God does.

_____

_____

_____

_____

Sorrow –

Worldly sorrow produces self-hate, self-loathing, and self-harm. How has this sorrow hurt you?

_____

_____

_____

Godly sorrow produces a God-change in direction. Feeling the way God feels about your dragon.

_____

_____

Meditation

"Make the most of your regrets; never smother your sorrow,
but tend and cherish it till it comes to have a separate and integral interest.
To regret deeply is to live afresh."

Henry David Thoreau

Ponder –

How can your sorrow/regrets help you to live afresh? Life always rises anew from the forest in the ashes after a fire.

_____

_____

_____

_____

_____

_____

_____

_____

Regrets can be crushing at times. Yet, regret shows a new way too. Mark out your new way here.

_____

_____

_____

_____

_____

Sorrow and guilt can drive you toward godly repentance. Throw yourself upon God's loving grace. Seek forgiveness in full confession of your addiction's bondage, damage, and activities. Sense God's love for you. See Jesus putting his arm around you, looking at your sin. He says, "Wow! That's a lot of sin! We need to work on this together. You see, I paid for all your sins on the cross. Really; your sins are gone. You are free from it. You just need to claim your freedom."

Now, we must get you to realize the freely loved and valued person that you are. We will take these next steps together. Let's begin because, "There is no condemnation for those who belong to Christ Jesus. And because you belong to him, the power of the lifegiving Spirit has freed you from the power of sin that leads to death." (Romans 1:1-2).

Prayer:

Oh, God,
My sorrow has slayed me repeatedly.
Worldly sorrow leaves me dead inside.
It makes me hate myself. At times I loathe your creation; me.
It makes me run from You. It makes me hide from those who love me.
Most of all it makes me hide from me.
Help me to see my sin – dragon the way you see it in my life.
Give me your sorrow over my sin.
Help me repent and turn from this stuff.
In your sorrow, there is no regret. I want to live without regret.

So Be It! – Amen.

Week # 17

*"And even when you ask, you don't get it because **your motives are all wrong** – you want only what will give you pleasure."*

James 4:3

*"Don't worry about anything; **instead**, pray about everything. **Tell God what you need**, and **thank him for all he has done**. <u>Then you will experience God's peace</u>, which exceeds anything we can understand. His peace will guard your hearts and minds as you live in Christ Jesus."*

Philippians 4:6-7

*"**Prayer** doesn't just change things - it **changes us**. If we are diligent in seeking God, slowly and surely we become better people."*

Joyce Meyer

*"Anything is a blessing which **makes us pray**."*

C. H. Spurgeon

Tell God What You Need!

It's that simple. Just tell God what you need at the time you need it. Every time you find yourself tempted, tell God, "God I am really worried about …" or, "God, I want to look at porn again. I want another drink. I want to huff. I want to snort. I want to shoot up. I mean, I really want it. This is not good for my family or me, and it brings sorrow to You. Give me your heart here, God, help me."

As a person struggling with anger daily, James learned to pray effectively every time he felt angry. He told me, "I wake up angry every day. Every time I find myself beginning to burn with irritation deep down inside, I pray. I say, 'God the enemy (anger) is back. Quiet it down, please. Calm me inside right now.'" Sometimes he prayed aloud. Most times he prayed within himself. He prayed dozens of times every day until he gained victory and control over his anger. He learned connected, consistent, and content. And, you know what? Twenty years later, he still prays almost daily about that anger. But, he's able to control his anger now.

Another person shared, "I guess the reason I like my addiction so much, is because it's the only thing that loves me." This revealed a deficit in his life. His prayer went something like, "God I am lonely again, and want to be loved. I need to be loved. I want someone to be interested in me. I feel empty and want to return to my addiction. But, my addiction is not real love. Your love and plan for my life is real. Help me to see that I am loved by you. You are real."

Thank God For what He's Done

Gratitude is the second essential to effective praying. The Bible encourages an attitude of thankfulness in all situations: "In everything give thanks: for this is the will of God in Christ Jesus concerning you." (1 Thessalonians 5:18 KJV)

While praying about everything and thanking God in everything, we learn gratitude. Thank God for your struggles. Struggling, forces you to look for help beyond yourself. Thank God for your losses, too. In loss, one appreciates possession. Thank Him for the events driving you to turn away from your destructive addiction. Thank Him for forgiveness, both God's and others. Thank Him for your struggle. The struggle helps you see your problem. It's helping you deal with it. Give thanks for every good thing around you. See the good stuff in your world. Thank God for forgiveness. Thank Him for His love, for His compassion, and for His mercy. Thank God for the second, third, and umpteenth start overs. **Gratitude is the secret.**

This is a huge struggle for many of us living in first world cultures, especially in the United States. Our consumer society conditions us to believe that my needs, wants, and desires supersede every other consideration around me. What I want is primary in my life, and everyone else's for that matter. I can only be thankful for the things I like. My life focuses only on me, and only on the stuff I want. Living in this dimension demotes gratitude. Gratitude becomes elusive and self-focused.

As you tell God your needs, learn to find gratitude in that same need. **Yes, be thankful for your struggle with addiction.** That is correct. It your addiction that has you focused on this very page. Addiction helps you see you need for others and God.

Express gratitude for the struggle, "Thank You, God, for my struggle with _____." In learning to value the good stuff of life, we learn to appreciate and enjoy living. Now, ask yourself, **"When was the last time I really gave thanks for anything?"**

Boundaries –

How Prayer-Strong are your boundaries? What Prayer-Practices can strengthen your walls?

_____

_____

_____

_____

_____

_____

_____

_____

Accountability –

What does your prayer time look like with your accountability team? How do you pray?

_____

_____

_____

_____

How can you strengthen your prayer during your time together? Do you pray at all?

_____

_____

_____

_____

Confession – (To agree about a thing, reveal it, or expose a secret)

What personal reflections do your confessions reflect in prayer?

_____

_____

_____

_____

_____

_____

_____

Knowledge –

What do you know about prayer? Talk simply and openingly about your prayer practices.

_____

_____

_____

_____

_____

_____

How might you increase your personal interactions and communication with God?

_____

_____

_____

_____

_____

Sorrow –

Where does sorrow fit into your conversations with God? Write out a sorrow-prayer here.

_____

_____

_____

_____

_____

Now, write out a joy-prayer here! How has regret breathed new life and hope into you?

_____

_____

_____

_____

_____

_____

Meditation

"For prayer is nothing else than being on terms of friendship with God."

Saint Teresa of Avila

Ponder –

Think about your friendship with God. Describe your friendship.

_____

_____

_____

_____

What are some of the marks of friendship? A True friend is:

_____

_____

_____

_____

_____

Read about some friends of God in the Bible:

Jesus – "Now you are my friends, since I have told you everything the Father told me." John 15:15

God – "Since we were restored to friendship with God by the death of his Son while we were still his enemies, we will certainly be delivered from eternal punishment by his life." Romans 5:10

Abraham – "Abraham believed God, and God counted him as righteous because of his faith." He was even called the friend of God." James 2:23

Moses – ". . . the LORD would speak to Moses face to face, as one speaks to a friend." Exodus 33:11

How can you be God's friend?

_____

_____

_____

_____

_____

Prayer:

God,
Help me see you standing next to me.
Your arm around me as we both look at my sin.
You say, "That my friend is a lot of sin."
I look down in despair.
But, you reply, "We are going to work on it together.
You and me.
I'm going to help you get through this.
Over this.
And, beyond this.
If you will just trust me,
And draw near to me."

So Be It! – Amen.

Week # 18

*"You can pray for anything, and if you have faith, **you will receive it**."*

Jesus – Matthew 21:22

*"¹**Don't worry** about anything: instead,*
*²**pray** about everything.*
*³**Tell God** what you need,*
*and ⁴**thank him** for all he has done."*

Philippians 4:6

*"**Worry** does not empty tomorrow of its sorrow.*
*It **empties today of its strength**."*

Corrie Ten Boom

Scripture commands us to "to put off your old self, which belongs to your former manner of life and is corrupt through deceitful desires." (Ephesians 4:22 ESV) Closing avenues of addiction's access in your life is part of the "putting off" process.

However, when putting off things, a vacuum is created. Unless the emptiness created by removing an addiction is filled, failure often follows. When putting off bad practices, **you must put on something else in its place**. The Bible teaches, "Put on the new self, created after the likeness of God in true righteousness and holiness." (Ephesians 4:24 ESV) The process for renewing is sandwiched in between these two verses where the text says, "And to be renewed in the spirit of your minds." (Ephesians 4:23 ESV)

Renewal is the goal. Prayer – continual dependence upon God – renews. Eliminating addiction's exposure and replacing it with simple conversational prayer will focus your heart on God. **Tell God what you need**. Right here. Right now.

_____

_____

_____

_____

_____

_____

_____

_____

Now in Everything Give Thanks. Right here. Right Now.

_____

_____

_____

_____

_____

_____

_____

_____

Boundaries –

What worries crash against your boundaries' walls? Name them here. "I worry about . . ."

_____

_____

_____

_____

_____

_____

_____

Accountability –

God is your best accountability! How do you "tell God what you need?"

_____

_____

_____

Tell him what you need right now.

_____

_____

_____

_____

_____

_____

_____

_____

Confession – (To agree about a thing, reveal it, or expose a secret)

"Pray about everything . . ." What does this look like for you?

_____

_____

_____

_____

_____

_____

_____

_____

Knowledge –

What has God done for you?

_____

_____

_____

_____

_____

Thank him for all he's done.

_____

_____

_____

_____

_____

Gratitude changes Attitude

Sorrow –

Tell God right here about your sorrows and worries.

_____

_____

_____

_____

_____

Put off your worries right here and commit them to God. Tell him what you need.

_____

_____

_____

_____

_____

_____

_____

_____

_____

Meditation

"Worry pretends to be necessary but serves no useful purpose."

Eckhart Tolle

"Every tomorrow has two handles.
"We can take hold of it with the handle of anxiety or the handle of faith."

Henry Ward Beecher

"When you rise in the morning, give thanks for the light, for your life, for your strength. Give thanks for your food and for the joy of living. If you see no reason to give thanks, the fault lies in yourself."

Tecumseh

Ponder –

Which handle will you take hold of each day this week? The handle of anxiety or faith?

_____

_____

_____

_____

How does your worry pretend to be necessary?

_____

_____

_____

_____

_____

Prayer – Write your own prayer this week . . .

_____

_____

_____

_____

_____

_____

_____

_____

Week # 19

*"I plead with you to **give your bodies to God because** of all he has done
for you. Let them be a living and holy sacrifice—the kind he will find
acceptable. **This is truly the way to worship him.**

Don't copy the behavior and customs of this world, but let God
transform you into a new person by changing the way you think.
Then you will learn to know God's will for you,
which is good and pleasing and perfect."*

Romans 12:1-2

*"There is no other way to change something or someone for the better except to
occupy it first. The only person you can occupy is yourself. That is why the only
person who can change you for the better is you. Without your decision to change
and your commitment to change, you will not change."*

Gary Zukav

Boundaries –

What change in your thinking has your boundaries helped you accomplish?

_____

_____

_____

_____

What still needs to take place to help you defeat your dragon?

_____

_____

_____

Accountability –

Worship is the act of acknowledging the worth of something in your life. How do you worship? What holds high worth to you?

_____

_____

_____

_____

What is God worth to you?

_____

_____

_____

How much stronger is your accountability than before you started this journal?

_____

_____

_____

_____

Confession – (To agree about a thing, reveal it, or expose a secret)

Tell God about your greatest struggle.

_____

_____

_____

_____

_____

Knowledge –

How can transforming your thinking defeat your dragon? What does "transform" mean to you?

_____

_____

_____

_____

_____

_____

What is a "perfect will of God?"

_____

_____

_____

_____

_____

Sorrow –

How is your sorrow turning from despair into hope?

_____

_____

_____

_____

_____

How is your hope paving a new pathway of victory and joy over your dragon?

_____

_____

_____

_____

Meditation

"When we learn from experience, the scars of sin can lead us to restoration and a renewed intimacy with God."

Charles Stanley

"As you pray for the Holy Spirit to make you aware of thoughts that come into your mind that don't line up with God's Word, you'll begin to realize when those thoughts come and you can renew your mind with the Word."

Joyce Meyer

Ponder –

How many do you willfully surrender to your dragon?

_____

_____

_____

_____

_____

In comparison, how many times do you willfully surrender to God?

_____

_____

_____

_____

_____

How can you let God transform you into a new person by changing the way you think?

_____

_____

_____

_____

_____

Prayer – Write your own prayer this week. Begin it by saying, "God, through You, I can . . ."

_____

_____

_____

_____

_____

_____

_____

Week # 20

"... one final thing. **Fix your thoughts on what is true**, *and honorable, and right, and pure, and lovely, and admirable. Think about things that are excellent and worthy of praise.*

Keep putting into practice all you learned and received from me— everything you heard from me and saw me doing. ***Then the God of peace will be with you."***

Romans 12:1-2

"To enjoy good health, to bring true happiness to one's family, to bring peace to all, one must first discipline and control one's own mind. If a man can control his mind he can find the way to Enlightenment, and all wisdom and virtue will naturally come to him."

Buddha

Once, when I was teaching B.A.C.K.S. to a group of men, an older gentleman approached me after the fourth session. Like a sales agent, he barked out, "So, what's the bottom line here?" Looking for a quick fix, he wanted a simple and immediate remedy to evict his dragon from his heart's premises.

Philippians 4:8-9 is that bottom line. For many, this "one final thing" seems a difficult path to ascend. Yet, I maintain, the bottom line here is not that difficult. Look carefully.

Practice Daily Renewal

Paul in his letter to people in the church at Philippi concludes, "Keep putting into practice …" Here's the winning element. Practice brings proficiency. The Greek word for "practice" is "prasso" or "exercise." It means to be busy with or occupied by doing something.

Just as you may go to the fitness club or local YMCA, you must develop a routine of spiritual practice. Practicing bad habits brought you to where you are today. Practicing good and godly habits through prayerful dependence upon God will bring you to a better, more satisfying place. Remaining Prayer will go a long way toward helping you "keep putting into practice" the five-step BACKS approach in this book.

Fix your thoughts. The word "fix" is also translated in other versions of the Bible to "dwell" or "meditate." We have seen that dwelling word before. Where is your mental/spiritual dwelling? To dwell means to make one's dwelling or abode in a particular place. Begin to make your dwelling in better places than in past days.

What is true? Addiction does not offer true relationship. It is not satisfying. It does not portray life truthfully. Addiction is populated with unhappy people. Addiction is not harmless. It is not beautiful. It is not happy. It is not harmless; it's exploitive. It is not relational. Fill your mind and heart only with truth. Ask yourself, "Is this truthful?"

What is Honorable? This word means "respectful." Are your habits and actions respectful of God, others, and yourself? Addiction respects no one. Learn to respect every person created in God's image as God's child.

Is it Right? In every activity begin asking yourself, "Is this right?" You know the answer. Develop the habit of asking yourself this question every time you engage with media. Put your name in the beginning of the question, "_____, is this right?" Any hesitation other than an immediate "yes" is suspect.

Is this Pure? Pure, free from contaminants, is the idea here. Gold is only valuable if it's pure. While in South Africa years ago, we visited Gold Reef City Mines in Johannesburg. There we witnessed the process of melting down gold to remove all the impurities and contaminants from the raw ore. Intense heat ensures purity. Only after a rigorous process does gold become highly valuable. Purify your life.

Is this lovely? Again, in South Africa, among the English-speaking community, there exists a common word for approval. It is the word "lovely." When something was acceptable or pleasing, a person often responded, "That's lovely."

Is this Admirable? Can you speak well of your activity? Is what you're involved in something producing pride or guilt? Think About. This indicates a process. While the word "think" here carry several connotations, one of its meanings is "dwell." Here we are again; remaining and dwelling. What are you dwelling on right now? If it doesn't fall into the above categories, pray in asking for God's help. "God help me think about better things." The level of thought desired by God in our thought life is anchored in two expressions:

1. Is this excellent? The word "excellent" has a rich history, especially among ancient people. "The most articulated value in Greek culture is arête; the word actually has a meaning closer to 'being the best you can be,' or 'reaching your highest potential.'" God desires you to become the best you can be. He wants you to reach your highest potential, and he gives you the path to accomplish this in Philippians 4:6-8: thinking only on those things that bring excellence. God's heart for your life is so much bigger and more beautiful than where you are right now.

2. Is this praise-worthy? In our culture, much like the culture of Jesus' day, people seek praise from others. The Greeks were obsessed with praise. We should seek God's approval

124

only. This is the meaning of "praise-worthy." Does what you're thinking about bring praise to God, others, and to you?

Boundaries –

Fixing your thoughts upon the positive and pure builds strong boundaries. Work it through. What's the plan?

_____

_____

_____

_____

Fixing your thoughts upon what is true builds strong boundaries. How are your thoughts:

What's true?

_____

_____

What's pure?

_____

_____

What's lovely?

_____

_____

What's admirable?

_____

_____

Accountability –

Accountability requires practice. How are you putting into practice all you've learned?

_____

_____

_____

_____

_____

_____

Confession – (To agree about a thing, reveal it, or expose a secret)

Confession helps fix one's thoughts upon God. What does your confession sessions look like now?

_____

_____

_____

_____

_____

_____

Knowledge –

Keep putting into practice. Practice builds new habits. New habits changes thinking. New thinking transforms us into something better.

My New Practices _____

My New Habits _____

My New Thinking _____

_____

_____

My New Better _____

_____

_____

_____

_____

What is a "perfect will of God?"

_____

_____

_____

_____

_____

Sorrow –

From sorrow to peace . . .

Thinking about things that are excellent and worthy of praise replaces sorrow. What has replaced your sorrows with hope and a path forward?

_____

_____

_____

_____

_____

_____

_____

_____

_____

Meditation

*"We must not be wise and prudent according to the flesh.
Rather, we must be **simple**, **humble** and **pure**."*

Francis of Assisi

*"Means we use must be as **pure** as the ends we seek."*

Martin Luther King, Jr.

*"I have seen (as far as it can be seen) many persons changed in a moment from the spirit of horror,
fear, and despair to the spirit of hope, joy, peace; and from sinful desires, till then reigning over
them, to a pure desire of doing the will of God."*

John Wesley – Founder of Methodism

Ponder –

_____

_____

_____

_____

_____

What moves you about the above meditations?

_____

_____

_____

_____

_____

Prayer – Write your own prayer this week . . .

Connect the dots: **simple**…**humble**…**pure**…**desire**…your **life**.

Use the above five words in your prayer.

_____

_____

_____

_____

_____

_____

_____

_____

_____

_____

_____

_____

_____

Week # 21

"Then there was war in heaven. Michael and his angels fought against the dragon and his angels. And the dragon lost the battle, and he and his angels were forced out of heaven. This great dragon—the ancient serpent called the devil, or Satan, the one deceiving the whole world— was thrown down to the earth with all his angels."

Revelation 12:7-9

"Then I saw an angel coming down from heaven with the key to the bottomless pit and a heavy chain in his hand. He seized the dragon— that old serpent, who is the devil, Satan—and bound him in chains for a thousand years. The angel threw him into the bottomless pit, which he then shut and locked so Satan could not deceive the nations anymore until the thousand years were finished.
Afterward he must be released for a little while.

Revelation 20:1-3

"Then the devil, who had deceived them, was thrown into the fiery lake of burning sulfur, joining the beast and the false prophet. There they will be tormented day and night forever and ever."

Revelation 20:10

Ultimately, the dragon will be defeated. The Bible promises this! While the dragon holds incredible power now, the beast's reign upon this world is limited by God. It will ultimately come to an end. He is in fact already defeated. His end, coming in and culminating in a great battle in heaven, is assured.

The dragon is clearly on the losing side. His end results in a horrible, well-deserved, tormenting containment forever. Never again will the dragon enjoy freedom to harm and destroy. Never again will another child be harmed. Never again will disease ravage a healthy body. Never again will temptation approach us. Evil will cease. Only goodness will remain. With the dragon gone, so will its ruinous powers cease. He is finished forever! Good news! Great news! Encouraging news!

Here's more good news. Your dragon possesses this very moment only the power you extend to it. When you drop your boundaries, the dragon feeds off you. Pulling away from your dragon and learning to resist its presence deprives it of power. "Resist the devil, and he will flee from you" (James 4:7). God's power is available to you. If you choose to leverage God's power through His Son Jesus Christ, victory is yours. Three great promises of hope prevail when nestled in God's person:

> But you belong to God, my dear children. You have already won a victory over those people because the Spirit who lives in you is greater than the spirit who lives in the world (1 John 4:4).

> For every child of God defeats this evil world, and we achieve this victory through our faith (1 John 5:4).

> We know that God's children do not make a practice of sinning, for God's Son holds them securely, and the evil one cannot touch them (1 John 5:18).

Promise number one states, "You've already won the victory." Success is yours. **You only need to grasp it**.

Promise number two says "God's Spirit dwelling within you ensures victory." God's Spirit guarantees success. Paul writes to the Galatians, "So I say, let the Holy Spirit guide your lives. Then you won't be doing what your sinful nature craves" (Galatians 5:16).

The third promise is victory's immanency. Victory is yours right now, today, this very moment. Notice the words, "He cannot touch you." **Think about that for just a moment.** <u>Unless you allow it, the dragon cannot touch you.</u> The torments of your addictions, hold zero power over you unless you empower the dragon. What's the bottom line? How is success guaranteed? What does it take to overcome addiction in your life? Triumph depends upon this one pivotal question, "Do you belong to Jesus Christ?" Belonging is everything. Without belonging, you are crippled. In belonging there is hope:

> "So now there is no condemnation for those who belong to Christ Jesus. And because you belong to him, the power of the life-giving Spirit has freed you from the power of sin that leads to death" (Romans 12:1-2).

No condemnation. The word "condemnation" is courtroom language. It's the idea of sentencing one to a prison term. It's time to get out of jail. It's time to throw open your prison door. It's a prison cell confining you to a life of defeat, guilt, destruction, and unhappiness. Embrace faith this very moment. Perhaps your first step is to put your faith and trust in Jesus Christ alone. His life-giving Spirit will free you from the power of your sin. Putting your full faith in Jesus Christ brings belonging. This is the promise of Scripture:

> "Therefore, since we have been made right in God's sight by faith, we have peace with God because of what Jesus Christ our Lord has done for us. Because of our faith, Christ has brought us into this place of undeserved privilege where we now stand, and we confidently and joyfully look forward to sharing God's glory" (Romans 5:1-2).

If you've never put your faith in Christ Jesus, may I encourage you to do so now? A simple prayer of faith, depending on Jesus, is the beginning of change. Simply pray,

"Dear God, my need for You is great. My addiction is greater. My desire is for You. This very moment, I put my total faith in You alone. I begin a new life in You starting right now. Change me into the person of excellence You've created me to become. Thank You for Your love."

In Jesus Christ, all kinds of eternal processes begin now in your life. One new process is re-creation. "This means that anyone who belongs to Christ has become a new person. The old life is gone; a new life has begun!" (2 Corinthians 5:17).

If you've enjoyed a relationship with Christ for a period, that process still lives within you regardless of your failings. Christ still lives within you. The process of re-creation was halted because of your choices apart from God's image for your life. Perhaps, it's time to redirect your life to God. A simple prayer:

God, I'm where I'm at because of my own fault. Sorry. I've really messed up. Please forgive me, Father. Thank You for not giving up on me. Thank You for loving me. Thank You for second, third, fourth, and more chances. Take this tainted person before You. I commit my life to You. I give my body, mind, and spirit to You. Create in me a clean heart, God. Renew a right spirit within me. Let me experience the joy once again of knowing You. Help me, oh God, to reflect Your excellence through me to those around me.

So be it – Amen.

Strengthen your boundaries. Put your B.A.C.K.S. into it. The tools are before you. Master them. Build and establish your boundaries. Strong accountability provides safety. Confession redeems the heart. Knowledge brings clear understanding. And, godly sorrow brings your soul and God together. Put that dragon back behind its own wall never to cross your boundary again.

From Boundaries – 5 Steps to Getting Your Life BACK by Don Mingo, Faithway Publishers. Pages 175-179.

Boundaries –

How does the reality of the Great Dragon's End help give you a boundary of hope?

_____

_____

_____

_____

_____

_____

How could this reality give those around you hope?

_____

_____

_____

_____

_____

How will you defeat your own dragon? What's your plan?

_____

_____

_____

_____

_____

Accountability –

How might putting your full faith / trust in God help you in your struggles?

_____

_____

_____

_____

_____

Confession – (To agree about a thing, reveal it, or expose a secret)

Confess that your perspectives have focused less on God and more on your dragon.

_____

_____

_____

_____

_____

Knowledge –

The Great Dragon's End finalizes in containment and destruction. How does this knowledge help you? Hope is Yours! Victory is Yours! Go back and read the above Bible verses.

_____

_____

_____

_____

_____

Sorrow –

For too long you've lived in the shadows of Sorrow's dragon. Flee those shadows and run and hide in the Shadow of God!

> *"Those who live in the **shelter** of the Most High*
> *will find rest in the **shadow** of the Almighty."*

Psalm 91:1

135

About the Author

Dr. D. J. Mingo spent over twenty years in Africa with his wife Kathy raising their three sons. Pastoring, counseling, and assisting South Africans with varieties of challenges help build B.A.C.K.S.' formative process to help people. Addictions plague all people from every culture.

Don is a professional Life Coach, Personal, Group, Leadership, and Missionary Coach. He also holds several certifications and training in Critical Incident Stress Management, Chaplaincy, Trauma Care, Grief Care, Depression Recovery, Fire Fighting, and other disciplines. His greatest passion is helping God's people live life as God intended; abundantly.

Don and Kathy currently travel extensively helping Christian missionaries, pastors, and leaders in almost any capacity requested.

Don, and his wife Kathy, currently offer coaching and care for pastors, missionaries, multi-cultural workers, and those serving in the church. Their motto is:

"Helping leaders survive and thrive in ministry serving longer and stronger."

More information is available at:

www.M2MCare.org / www.donaldmingo.com / Facebook: M2MCare
Twitter: M2MCare / Instagram: M2MCare

Other books by Don Mingo

Boundaries – 5 Steps to Getting Your Life Back. Helping people overcome addictions with God's help. Faithway Publishers, Available on Amazon in paperback and Kindle.

Life Boundaries – Balancing Career, Marriage, Relationships, and the Important Stuff of Life. Available on Amazon in paperback and Kindle.

Son Risings – Discovering and Caring for the Real You. Available on Amazon in paperback and on Kindle.

Notes

[1] APA (6th ed.) Tyndale House Publishers. (2004). Holy Bible: New Living Translation. Wheaton, Ill: Tyndale House Publishers. All Scripture is from the NLT unless otherwise cited.
[2] Ibid.